Early Morning Light

Volume 1

Communion of Light Book of Quotations Series

Early Morning Light, Volume 1

Early Morning Light
Volume 1

A Communion of Light Book of Quotations

Frank W. Butterfield

Butterfield Imprint
MMXV

ISBN-10: 1508493596
ISBN-13: 978-1508493594

First publication: February 2015

Printed in the United States of America.

Love never ends.

Your ability to have what you want is directly related to your willingness to not have it.

You're powerful creators.
There's no doubt
about that.
And the single tool that
you use is the organizing
principle of the Universe
which is what all of
Source Energy uses in
order to expand.

Don't be fooled into believing that what you see is what is real. Your focus upon what you are wanting is indeed causing the universe around you to shift and line up with what you are expecting.

You are source energy

expanding and evolving

through the very desires

that rise up within you.

You are here, now.

This is where you are.

This is where your power is.

And your power is

in your decision.

We recommend decisions

that feel better

in their making.

When you are taking inspired action, the road rises up to meet you.

As you take a breath, from one moment to the next, it will become increasingly more obvious that, no matter how you got here, this is the new beginning.

The plain fact is that you are a magnificent being of light who has taken physical form for a short while for the pure joy of it all.

Being successful is a given.

You already are a

tremendous success.

Your presence in physical

reality is proof of that.

Wherever you are, whatever may be happening, you always have an opportunity to reach for a thought that feels better by simply taking a deep breath and opening up to what is right in front of you.

You really do always know what you are doing.

Every day is a new beginning. This happens every morning when you awake from your non-physical adventures and come back to this magical playground you have created for the fun and delight of it.

You are abundant, wealthy and rich right now because of your imagination, not because of your circumstance.

This creation known as your body is astonishing. And we do highly recommend that you let it be the amazing, wonderful, delicious creation that it actually is.

The love that you are is unconditional. This reality is your playground. Anything is possible. What feels better to create today?

As vast as your reality

appears to be,

it is but

a single thought

in your mind.

Our suggestion is that you go out and about amongst your amazing thoughts, these creations of yours, and get your hands dirty and fall all over the ways in which you have decided to create.

Anytime any voice within you asks, "Is it enough?" The answer is always the open-ended answer, "Yes it's enough. Am I doing it right? Yes, I'm doing it right. Do I know what I'm doing? Yes, I know what I'm doing."

There is great risk in choosing the easy path. You might actually feel better and that might annoy some other people.

You are vibrating at the rate of freedom already. The question is whether you are aware of it or not.

When you let the Universe
of your thoughts take
charge of the arranging of
physical reality, you are
allowing yourself
to actually have
what you actually want.

When we speak on behalf of

your non-physical friends,

your helpers, as we do here,

what we are always saying

is the same thing:

"We love you

unconditionally."

We invite you

to do the same.

The unconditional love that underwrites your experience is literally everywhere, in everything, and in all your relationships.

You are the one who has created this moment. And, in this moment, you are in the right place, with the right people, at the right time, and in the right way.

Your life is a journey organized by Infinite Intelligence and underwritten by Unconditional Love. Anything is possible and there will be no loss.

When we talk about our love for you, know that it is the same love you have for yourself.

It is the same love that you are.

This love is unconditional and knows no limits yet expands constantly.

When is now?

We think that is a very good

question to ask indeed.

The very thing that you think is holding you back contains within it the magnificence that you will undoubtedly use to liberate yourself.

*Look around you, for you
will see that you are already
in the fullness of the
manifestation of your
heart's desire.*

Whatever you are looking for has already found you, so you can actually relax if you want to do so.

It is helpful to remember that you have everything that you want already and that you are a perfect vibrational match to every single thing that is going on, whether you like what is going on or not.

Bang the drum of having it, whatever it is that you want, and let the Universe handle the details for you.

If you take a moment and think about the positive contrast that is showing up in your life right now, you might very well be amazed at how you are already living the life of your dreams.

We are here to help you surrender to the fullness of what you have already created.

Today is that day that you have been promising to yourself that you would finally allow what you are actually wanting.

There's nothing wrong with where you are. The way through any situation is to realize that this is the case and thus allow yourself to emerge into the fullness of what you're wanting.

The body itself is not just the physical body, it's actually a non-physical entity that has a physical form.

When we are talking about love, we mean the love that exists naturally as a result of the fact that you are present.

How many times will you push against who you are? Likely it will be many and likely it will go on for a while. However, you can change your mind right now and let what-is be what it is and know that all is well.

More of what you are wanting is available right now through the thought that feels better.

We invite you to let yourself realize the magnificence that you already are.

Making and trying and getting and pushing is what used to work.

Allowing, receiving, opening is what you now know really works.

This is so simple.

Today we suggest that you finally face reality and make the decision for free-flowing abundance. For your true nature is one of limitlessness.

It's a radical approach to say plainly that you are creating your reality.

Not everyone will agree with this.

Not everyone need agree with this.

Only you will know if this is relevant to you.

Now is the time and this is the place and here is where you are.

Let everyone help you, even the ones who say no.

This is all a lot simpler and easier than you may believe right now.

Putting yourself at the heart of the unconditional love that is manifesting through you is right where you actually already are.

One moment is all that is required to feel better.

The entire universe is quite literally helping you out in ways so powerful and so immediate that you can't possibly know them all but you can certainly relax into this delicious awareness.

Whenever you look around and take stock of what you see, you have an opportunity to find all manner of things and people and situations to appreciate. They are all around you, right now.

It really can be quite fun to have more and more money. And, you may also notice some contrasting thoughts about having more and more money. And, that's OK.

Your body is always in

perfect and exquisite

alignment with you, who

you are, and who

you are becoming.

It's never upset with you.

It never wonders why you're

doing this and

not doing that.

If you insist on going

upstream, it is our

suggestion that you stand

behind your choice

consciously and

say to yourself,

"I am choosing to do this."

There is within you

limitless power.

This is not something
we say by rote:
"Follow the thought that
feels better."
It is our way of handing
back to you the
keys to the kingdom.

Whatever you are wanting is exactly what you are wanting, and that is perfect.

When you realize that you don't have to eat your peas before you have your ice cream, then you are free to make choices that make sense and feel better to you from where you are.

If you want security, turn within, focus on your ability to create what you want and rely upon that.

Because that is highly reliable.

When your imagination runs wild, you begin to sort things out within your vibrational reality instead of trying to get your physical reality to conform or shift into what you are wanting.

So much of your resistance to the what-is derives from the false assumption that love is a doing and that you must love everything in a doing sort of way.

It might feel better, as it were, to just sit in what it is that you are experiencing. It's only when you are having resistance to what you are experiencing when you really are having any trouble.

The very people who do not like what you are creating are the ones who are helping you create more brilliantly.

Helpers will help you magnify what you're wanting through their reminders to you that, not only can you have what you want, but that you have the desire to have it and that must make it inevitable.

This world is completely of your making.

You created it and populated it and it reflects different thoughts and beliefs that you hold and have held in the past.

It is more like a hologram than anything else.

We invite you to look for more and more of what you are wanting as already being integrated in your life. We invite you to imagine saying,
"I have what I want and it is just right for me and quite normal."

You can't control the situation. You can't change who this person who is, or how he acts, or what he does, or what he says.
All that you can really do is just decide:
"I'm going to have a better experience for myself."

Sexuality is just one of the many unique characteristics that each of you bring to the collective table.

It is through this uniqueness and diversity that you blend together a very delicious and truly amazing world.

What do you want to be right about today? We recommend that you be right about how conditions are temporary and always getting better and how everything always works out wonderfully.

You are powerful creators

and are creating the reality

you experience.

What do you want more of?

Bring your focus to that and

watch it blossom

and expand.

You didn't come here

to get rich.

You came here for

the fun of it.

But you think that getting

rich would be a lot of fun.

Well then, by gosh, by golly,

go get rich.

When you are basking and reveling, you never need to go faster or do more. It's all just right at that moment.

This physical universe that you inhabit is entirely of your creation.
This is what we mean when we say that you are creating your own reality.

The more you try to fix your brokenness the more brokenness you're going to observe.

Reach for a thought that feels better in its thinking, words that feel better in their speaking, or actions that feel better in their doing and you are on your way.

It's that simple.

Even if you're not writing it down, even if you're just thinking it through, you're translating a non-physical vibrational reality into a more solid physically-oriented physical reality.

The way you've been trained to be considerate of others is to decide beforehand what it is that they want and then accommodate yourself to that.
But that's just a wild guess.

There really is no end to what you can imagine and, as a result, no end to what you can create.

Finding yourself at the very center of your experience is finding yourself right where you are.

When you are thinking about the world around you, it is helpful to remember that everything happening is an extension of the Unconditional Love that you are.

Open to the heart of who you are, which is simply unconditional love manifesting in form.

Today is that amazing day.

You no longer have to wait.

Knowing that this moment is the right one and that this place is the right one can carry you a long way into the peace and freedom that you actually are.

Your thoughts are your creations and they want to expand and evolve away from you.

You do this normally with thoughts you like.

It's only the thoughts you don't like that you squirrel away.

There is no place that you can go where love is not.

If the thought feels better from where you are, then you are on the right track for the fullness and deliciousness of all that you are creating.

Contrast arises naturally in every situation, no matter what it is that you are thinking about or where it is that you are pointing your focus of concentration consciousness.

You are living your magical life right now.

When you see something that you find beautiful, it is a reminder of your powerful alignment with Source, because how you are seeing what you are seeing is in the same manner that Source sees you.

89

It is to compound a misdemeanor into a felony to pretend that you are being forced to take any action, since that is never the case. You are always choosing where you go next.

One of the fastest ways we know to let go of something unwanted, whether it's an experience, a memory, an aspect of a relationship, or a tangible object is to look it squarely in the face and realize that you are the one who has created this.

Find the next thought that feels better and you are on your way to more and more of what you are wanting.

How you got here is never that important.

Where you go from here, well, you have complete control over that.

Just follow the feeling of the idea of what is wanted and it will lead you there.

Reveling feels like what happens when you are dancing and your feet are moving with the beat and the music keeps getting better and better and you feel so connected and in tune with life.

*Your physical universe is
more like a hologram than
anything else.
Its substance is very real
and can be measured but its
structure rests on very
powerful beliefs.
These beliefs are not
permanent.*

You decide to allow what you have powerfully summoned forth. And in that decision, you are stepping back and giving the Universe room to move on your behalf.

You can go for years and years of ignoring your intuition and then turn to it when you are ready and you will find it providing you with exactly the next step in precisely the way that is right for you.

You didn't come here to deal with the burdens of the past. You came here to create the reality that you are dreaming of.

Do you want to connect with the one who is easy to be with, who adores you, who is open to the relationship, who wants to spend time with you? Or do you want to connect with the one who is distant and difficult and not very interested in the you that you are?

You'll never be able to please everyone and that's a very good thing indeed.

It can be quite fun to let yourself have more and more of what you're wanting in ever-more delicious ways. Our suggestion is that you not wait to do so.

Cultivate the thoughts that you DO like to think; that you like to think, that you like to think.

We just want to say that over and over and over again.

When you say that,

"All is well,"

what you are saying is that

where you are

is perfect.

The decision for health is simply the decision to connect with, be aware of, and have the full benefit of being immersed in the powerful wellbeing that has been your body's experience since its conception.

If you know how to think about what you feel, you can create anything you want with ease.

You did not come here for the oneness of it all, for that is what you are already.

Find a way to feel better from where you are. Improved vibration means improved conditions. It really is that simple and that easy.

Well, the simplest thing we can say to you, and the most direct thing, and the most practical thing that we can offer you is to just decide that it's getting better.

It is important to remember that all emotions are valid because they represent movement from one vibrational state to another. They are signposts and we recommend paying attention to them.

*Your life is a dynamic thing
and you are only right here,
right now.*

There's nothing really here to learn. What you are doing, however, is you are remembering. And some of you remember through lessons, some of you remember through experience, and some of you remember by pondering.

There is nothing more delicious than listening for that voice within you as it speaks to you, in whatever way that may happen, and then moving forward in alignment.

We would say this and say it often, "I simply don't have the time to worry about my life or what's coming. I'm way too busy enjoying what I have right here and looking forward to more of the good stuff that's coming." We would say this a lot, in fact.

All that you are doing when you are imagining is affirming something that already exists.

What we love about you is your profound sense of knowing that you're right on the cusp of always understanding a bit more about who you really are and what that means in terms of the reality you are living in.

There are going to be things

that bridge the gap between

where you are and where you

want to be that help soothe

you and help move you there.

You don't have to task yourself

with finding

these bridges;

they will arise naturally.

Your intuition is simply the translation of how you are plugged in to Infinite Intelligence.

We're simply suggesting that you find ways to ascribe the most positive interpretation that you can give to the motives and to the actions and to the expressions that the people in your life bring to the table.

You are Source Energy

in form.

Bubbling delight is an active expression of love.

Basking feels like what happens when you go to the beach and you lay in the Sun and enjoy the sounds of children playing in the surf and birds telling each other about where the best fish are and you feel so relaxed and opened.

You created the physical universe you inhabit and have become very adept at blending this reality with everyone you know.

The decision for health is a metaphysical step that you can take to plug into the delightful experience of being at peace with your body in any situation or circumstance.

There is great power and satisfaction in the act of intentionally focusing on what you are wanting more of.

It's patently unfair to yourself to look back at the past and judge that you could have done better. You think you know that now through the positive contrast of this moment but you really didn't know it then.

Emotions are simply the vibrational indicators that tell you where you are in relationship to the thoughts you are thinking.

We want you to think about money in the same way as you think about running water. That money is something that really you can turn off and turn on as much as you want and there is an endless amount of it available to you.

Intuition flows constantly in response to your vibrational stance and always presents you with the next thought, word, or action that feels better from where you are right now.

As good as it is right now, and it really is very, very good indeed, it's going to be getting even better and better from here.

The plain fact is that you are a magnificent being of light who has taken physical form for a short while for the pure joy of it all.

When you feel as though you're heart is breaking, that is when a tremendous amount of possibility arises.

Every moment, you are living a in a bright new world. You didn't come here to deal with the reality constructed by your society and your culture. You didn't come here to deal with the burdens of the past. You came here to create the reality that you are dreaming of.

What we love about you is how you allow what you want to happen so beautifully.
This happens more than you tend to believe.

Engaging directly with the delicious vibration of what you are wanting and then allowing it to come into manifestation is always a very wonderful experience

Thoughts don't dissolve,

they evolve.

What we love about you is that you want to feel the power that always flows through you and that you want this, even when you feel the most powerless.

The key to having it quickly is to find what it is you are expecting this experience to feel like and to bring that feeling into this moment. In other words, don't wait to have what you're wanting.

When you realize, "There's this thing that's happening that I don't like."
That's the beginning of everything changing because you're realizing what is. Because you obviously don't like it and you can have it however you want it.

What you're really doing when you're working with any person, whomever they may be and in whatever role, is that you are offering them your love through your vision, through your opening, through your services and whatever you may be doing.

When it's going well, we recommend you milk the moment by basking in how delicious you feel.

Doing this creates more of it.

What we love about you is your insistence upon experiencing improved conditions around you.

You came here for the delight of sex, the taste of chocolate, the thousand colors of a sunset.

About Frank W. Butterfield

Frank W. Butterfield is a master channel who has helped thousands experience powerful shifts in consciousness through his delicious work with The Communion of Light, a group of non-physical beings who speak through him using a single voice.

Paul, as this voice is called, shares a consistent and powerful message of freedom that we create our reality and are not at the effect of it, that we can joyfully remember who we really are as these creators, and that life comes together much simpler and easier than we've taught ourselves to believe.

Frank travels internationally, sharing Paul's voice with groups and individuals, in person and online.

For more information:

communionoflight.com

Paul & The Communion of Light on Facebook:

facebook.com/CommunionOfLight

Printed in Great Britain
by Amazon

65587399R00088